I have a garden.

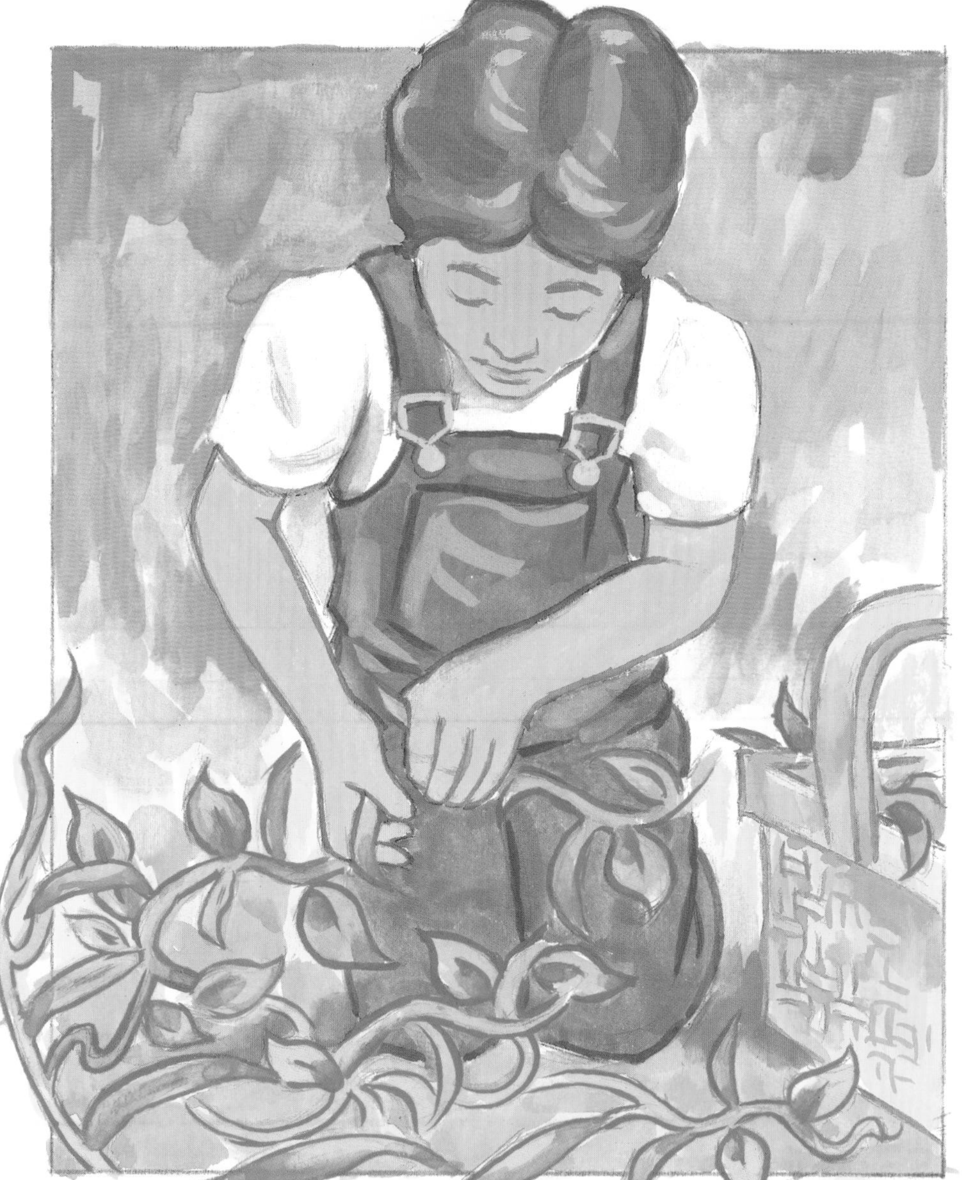

In my garden
I have green peas.

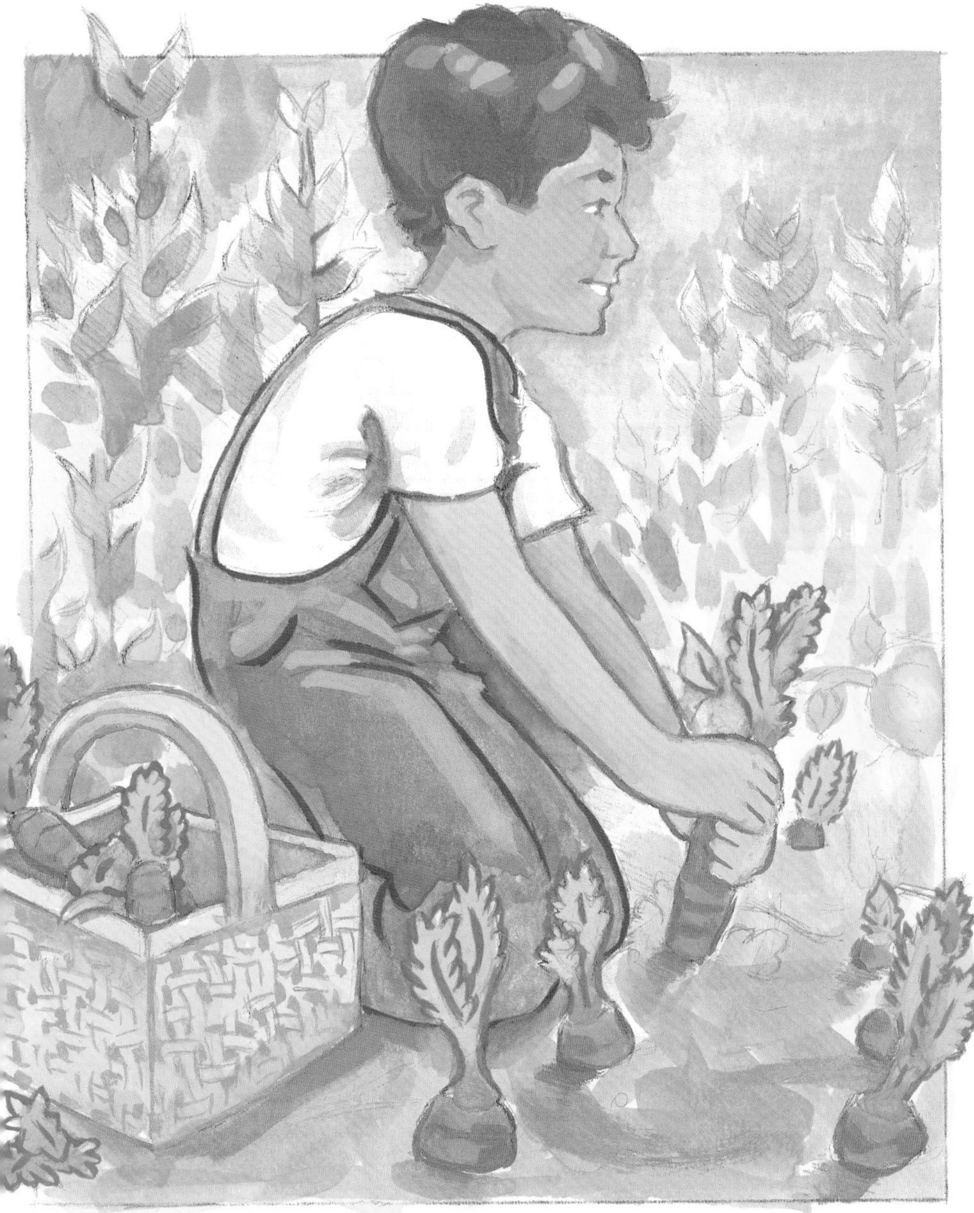

I have orange carrots.

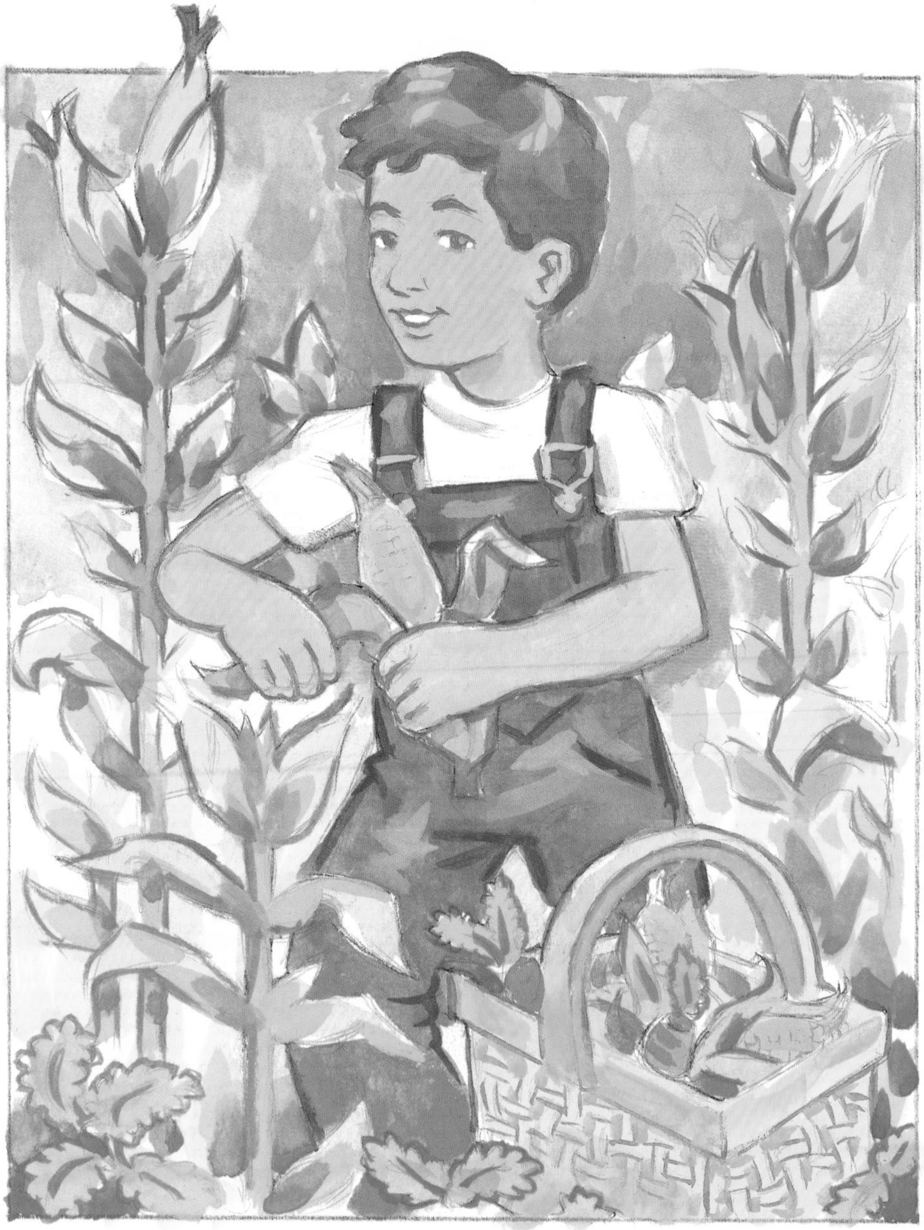

I have yellow corn.

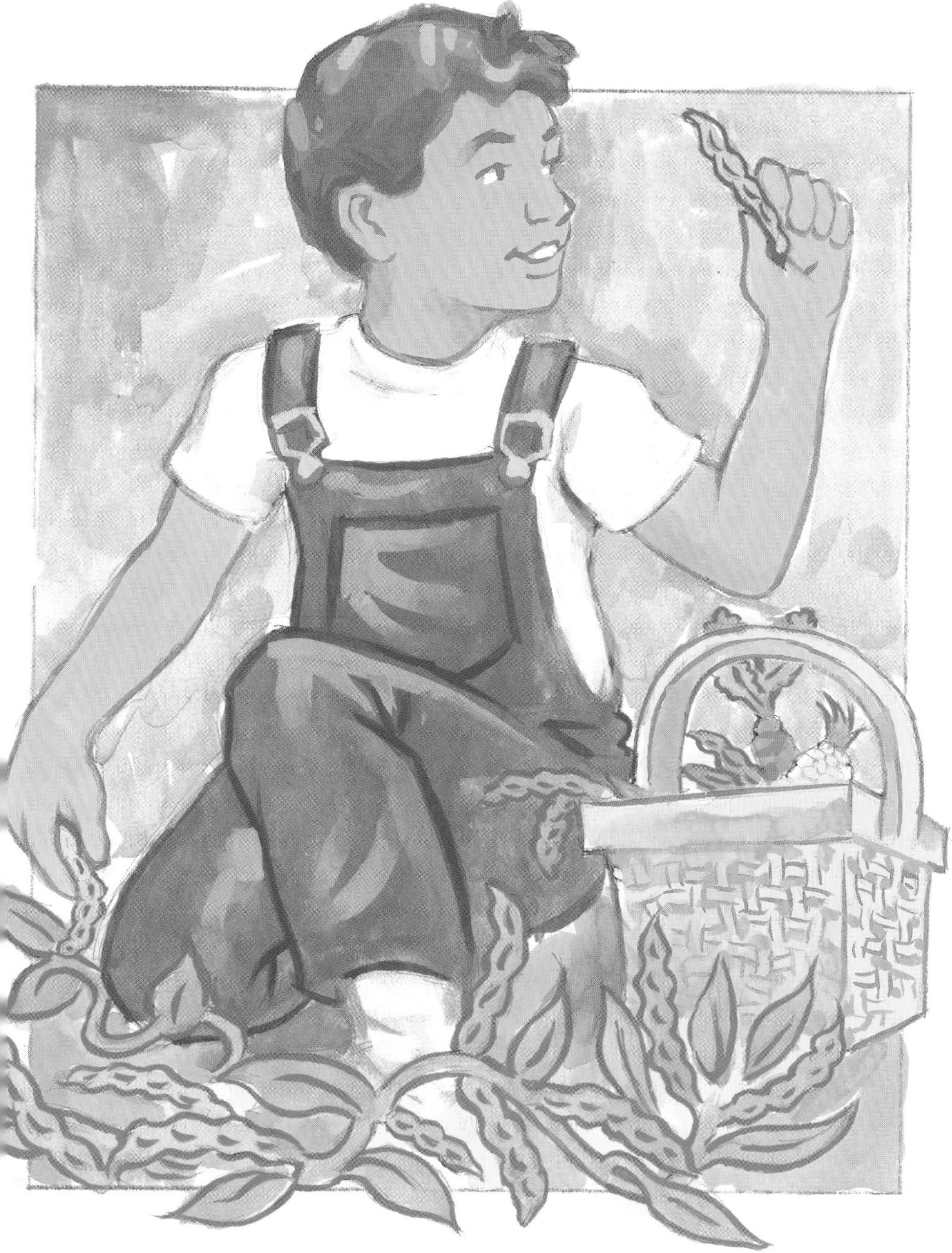

I have green beans.

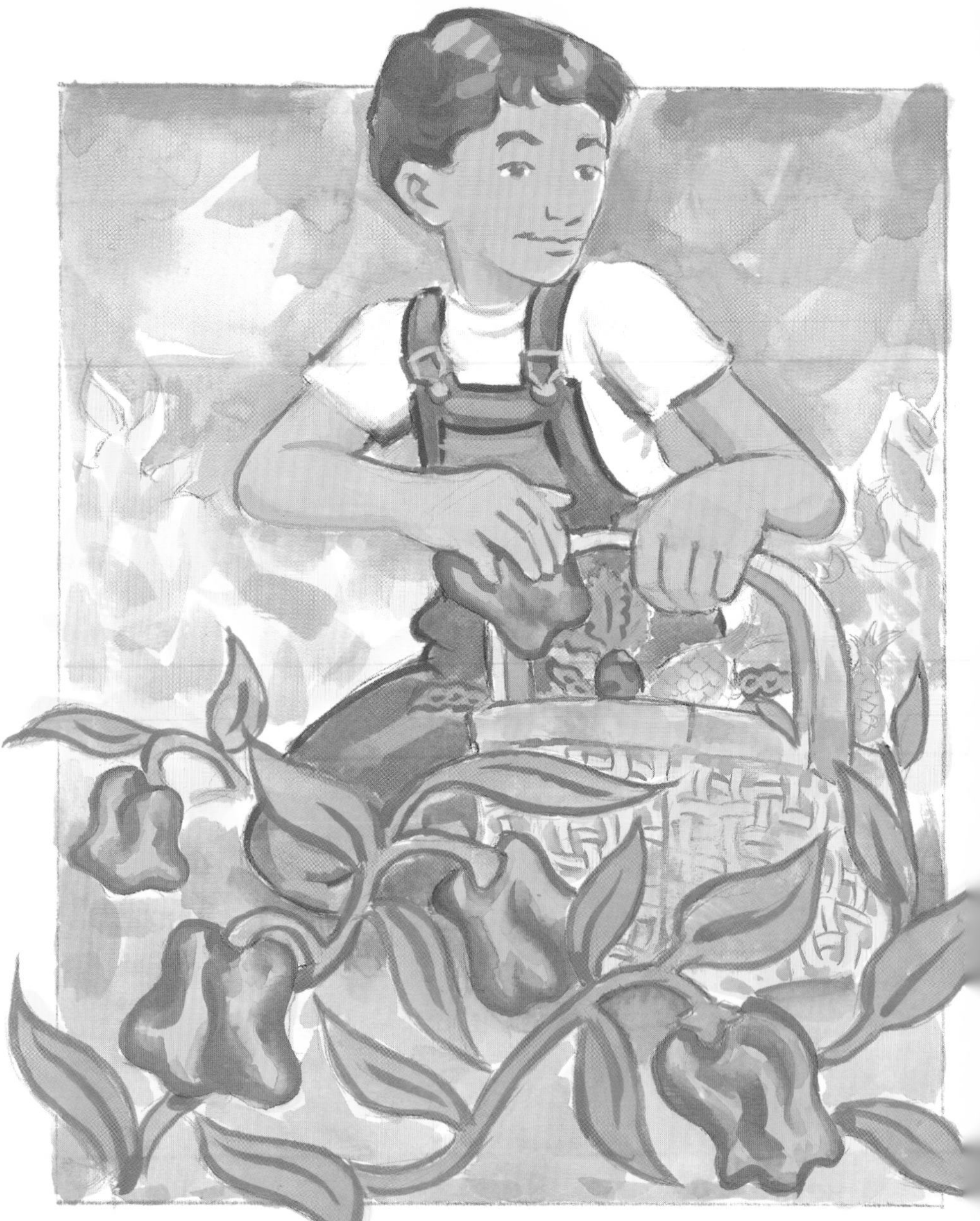

I have red peppers.

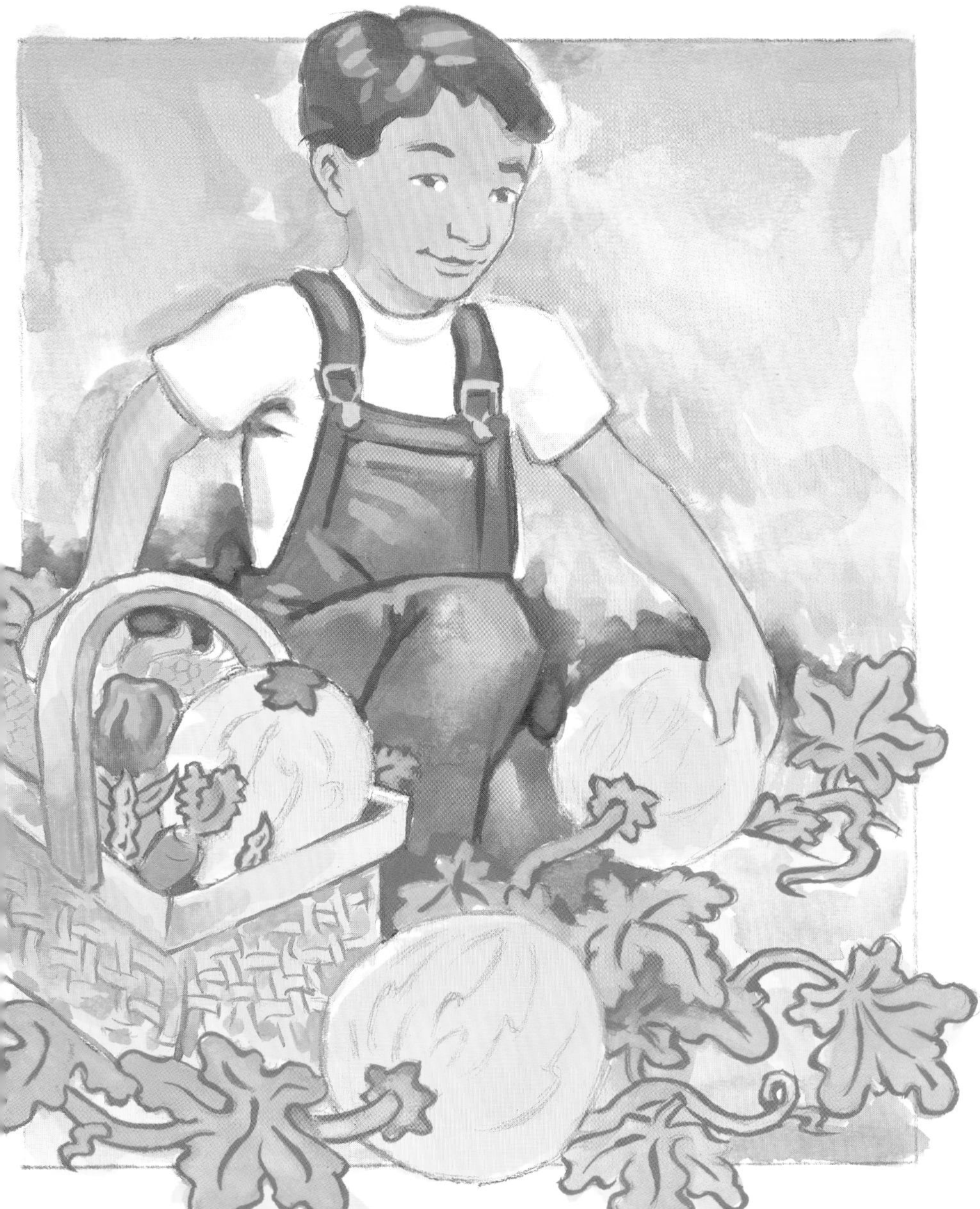

I have yellow squash.

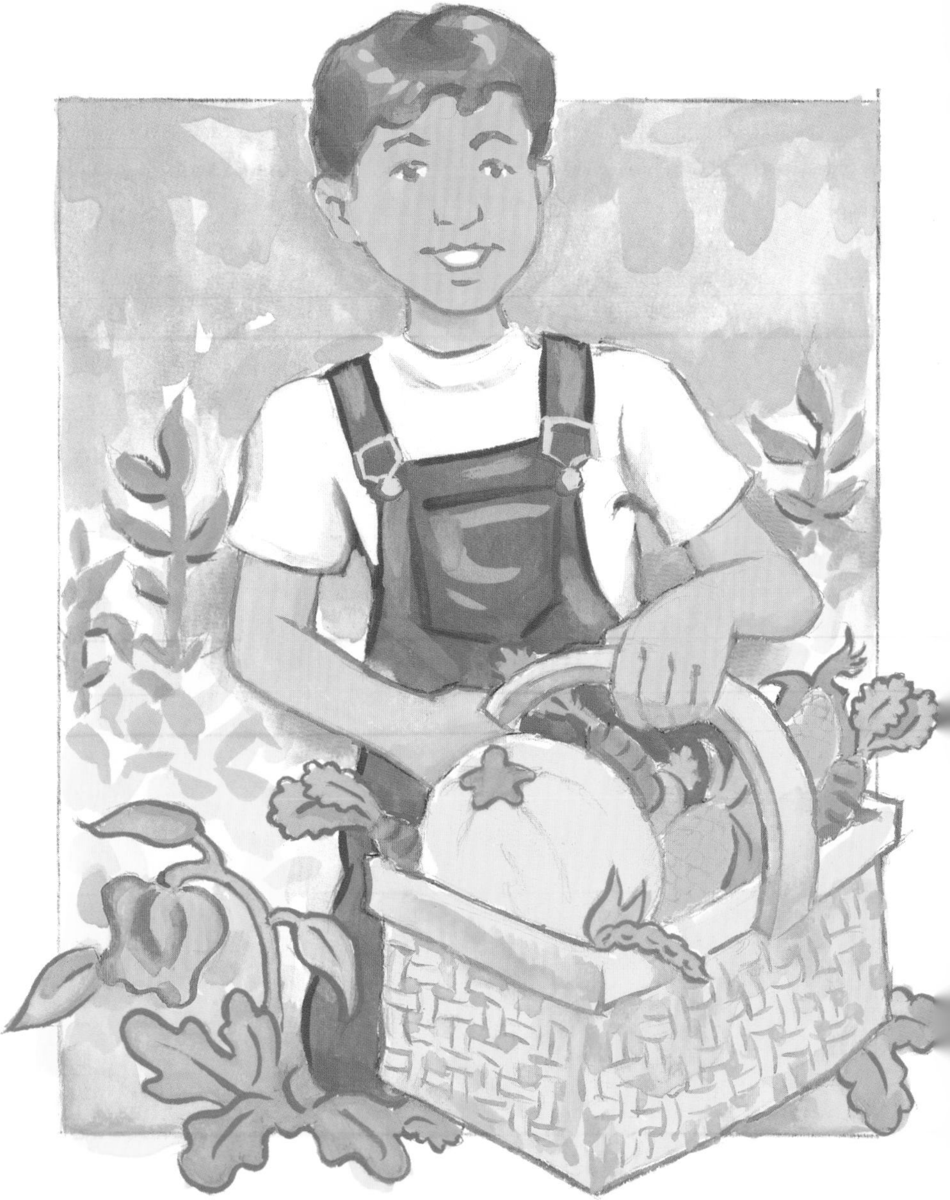

I have a colorful garden.